HERERO

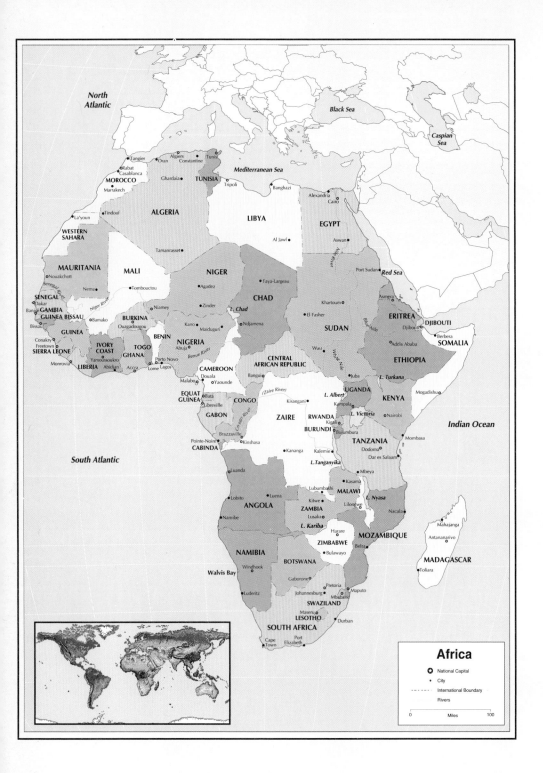

North
Atlantic

Black Sea

Caspian
Sea

Tangier
Algiers
Oran Constantine Tunis
Rabat
Casablanca
MOROCCO
Ghardaia
TUNISIA
Tripoli

Mediterranean Sea

Banghazi

Marrakech

La'youn
Tindouf

ALGERIA

LIBYA

Alexandria
Cairo

EGYPT

WESTERN
SAHARA

Tamanrasset

Al Jawf

Aswan

MAURITANIA

Nouakchott

MALI

NIGER

Faya-Largeau

Port Sudan

Red Sea

Nema
Tombouctou

Agadez

CHAD

Asmera

ERITREA

DJIBOUTI

SENEGAL
Dakar
Banjul GAMBIA
GUINEA BISSAU
Bissau

Niamey
Zinder
L. Chad

Kano
Maiduguri

Khartoum

El Fasher

SUDAN

Blue Nile

Djibouti
Berbera

Addis Ababa

SOMALIA

Bamako
Ouagadougou
BURKINA

Ndjamena

BENIN

Conakry
Freetown
SIERRA LEONE
Monrovia
LIBERIA

GUINEA

IVORY
COAST
Yamoussoukro
Abidjan

TOGO
GHANA
Accra

NIGERIA
Abuja

Benue River

Porto Novo
Lome Lagos

CAMEROON

Douala
Malabo
Yaounde

CENTRAL
AFRICAN REPUBLIC

Bangui

Wau

White Nile

Juba

ETHIOPIA

L. Turkana

UGANDA

Mogadishu

EQUAT
GUINEA
Bata
Libreville

CONGO

GABON

(Zaire River)

Kisangani

ZAIRE

RWANDA
Kigali
BURUNDI
Bujumbura

L. Albert

Kampala

L. Victoria

KENYA

Nairobi

Indian Ocean

Pointe-Noire
CABINDA

Brazzaville

Congo River

Kinshasa

Kananga

Kalemie

TANZANIA

Dodoma

Mombasa

Dar es Salaam

South Atlantic

Luanda

L.Tanganyika

Mbeya

Kasama

Lobito
Luena

Lubumbashi
Kitwe

MALAWI

L. Nyasa

ANGOLA

Namibe

ZAMBIA
Lusaka
L. Kariba

Lilongwe

Nacala

Harare

MOZAMBIQUE

ZIMBABWE
Bulawayo

Beira

Mahajanga

Antananarivo

MADAGASCAR

Toliara

NAMIBIA

Windhoek

BOTSWANA

Walvis Bay

Gaborone

Pretoria

Maputo

Luderitz

Johannesburg

Mbabane

SWAZILAND

Maseru
LESOTHO

Durban

SOUTH AFRICA

Cape
Town
Port
Elizabeth

Africa

✪ National Capital

• City

- - - International Boundary

Rivers

0   Miles   100

The Heritage Library of African Peoples

HERERO

Ada Udechukwu

THE ROSEN PUBLISHING GROUP, INC.
NEW YORK

For My In-Laws, Mr. B. Haidara and Mrs. S. Tall.

Published in 1996 by The Rosen Publishing Group, Inc.
29 East 21st Street, New York, NY 10010

First Edition

Manufactured in the United States of America

Library of Congress Cataloging-in-Publication Data

Udechukwu, Ada
    Herero / Ada Udechukwu.
      p. cm. — (The heritage library of African peoples)
    Includes bibliographical references and index.
    Summary: Discusses the history, culture, religion, traditions, and contemporary life of the Herero peoples living mainly in Namibia and Botswana.
    ISBN 0-8239-2003-8
    1. Herero (African people)—History—Juvenile literature.
2. Herero (African people)—Social life and customs—Juvenile literature. [1. Herero (African people)] I. Title. II. Series.
DT1558.H47U34 1995
968.8'00496399—dc20   95-40769
                                                      CIP
                                                          AC

Contents

INTRODUCTION

THERE IS EVERY REASON FOR US TO KNOW something about Africa and to understand its past and the way of life of its peoples. Africa is a rich continent that has for centuries provided the world with art, culture, labor, wealth, and natural resources. It has vast mineral deposits, fossil fuels, and commercial crops.

But perhaps most important is the fact that fossil evidence indicates that human beings originated in Africa. The earliest traces of human beings and their tools are almost two million years old. Their descendants have migrated throughout the world. To be human is to be of African descent.

The experiences of the peoples who stayed in Africa are as rich and as diverse as of those who established themselves elsewhere. This series of books describes their environment, their modes of subsistence, their relationships, and their customs and beliefs. The books present the variety of languages, histories, cultures, and religions that are to be found on the African continent. They demonstrate the historical linkages between African peoples and the way contemporary Africa has been affected by European colonial rule.

Africa is large, complex, and diverse. It encompasses an area of more than 11,700,000

square miles. The United States, Europe, and India could fit easily into it. The sheer size is an indication of the continent's great variety in geography, terrain, climate, flora, fauna, peoples, languages, and cultures.

Much of contemporary Africa has been shaped by European colonial rule, industrialization, urbanization, and the demands of a world economic system. For more than seventy years, large regions of Africa were ruled by Great Britain, France, Belgium, Portugal, and Spain. African peoples from various ethnic, linguistic, and cultural backgrounds were brought together to form colonial states.

For decades Africans struggled to gain their independence. It was not until after World War II that the colonial territories became independent African states. Today, almost all of Africa is ruled by Africans. Large numbers of Africans live in modern cities. Rural Africa is also being transformed, and yet its people still engage in many of their customs and beliefs.

Contemporary circumstances and natural events have not always been kind to ordinary Africans. Today, however, new popular social movements and technological innovations pose great promise for future development.

George C. Bond, Ph. D., Director
Institute of African Studies
Columbia University, New York

Herero women are famous for their distinctive long dress, seen here. The costumes are a unique blend of earlier Herero and nineteenth-century Western fashions, with modern touches added.

THE HERERO AND THEIR LAND

THE TERM HERERO REFERS TO A GROUP OF peoples who speak a common language. These are the Mbanderu, the Tjimba, the Himba, and the Herero. It is believed that they share a common origin, and their cultures are similar.

Today the Herero number about 107,000. Of these, 70,000 live in Namibia. Most of the others live in southern Angola and Botswana. Their language, Otjiherero, is part of the Bantu group of languages. There are three main dialects of the Herero language. Those Herero whose roots are in central northeastern Namibia speak Herero, while to the east of that region Mbanderu is spoken. Chimba is spoken by the Tjimba and Himba of the Kaokoveld and southern Angola.

In their early history, the Herero were nomadic cattle-herders, or pastoralists. The major-

ity of Herero now combine cattle-rearing with an agricultural lifestyle. They also keep other livestock, such as goats and sheep. Among the Herero and Mbanderu, wage-paying jobs in towns and cities are an alternative means of earning a living.

Today most Herero are in the north, central, and eastern parts of Namibia and in Botswana. Hereroland is flat and sandy, with permanent sand dunes in its western parts. The climate is typical of a semidesert region, with hot days and cold nights. Rainfall is low and ground water scarce. A few wide, shallow watercourses drain off seasonal flood water. The vegetation consists of low-lying shrubs.

The story of the Herero and their land is complex. Early records indicate that the ancestors of the Herero were part of a large group of Bantu-speaking people who began a great migration southward from central Africa about 1550. The migrating Herero left the main group and began to enter present-day Namibia from the northeast. At this point they split into two groups. One group crossed the Okavango River and moved into the Gobabis area; they became known as the Mbanderu, or the Eastern Herero. The other group crossed the Kunene River and settled in the Kaokoveld; today they identify themselves as Tjimba and Himba. In the Kaokoveld, dry hills and rugged mountain

The Herero and Their Land

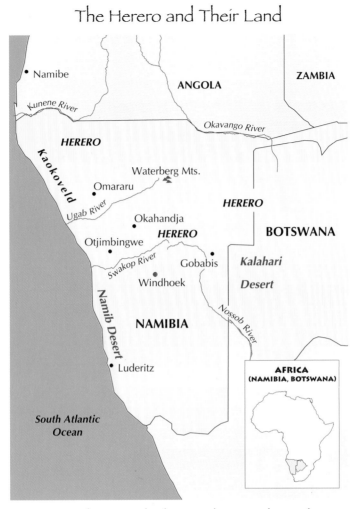

The Herero-speaking peoples live mostly in Namibia and Botswana. Herero in Botswana are known as Mbanderu, and the Herero-speakers in the Kaokoveld are the Himba and Tjimba.

ranges give way to the sand of the Kalahari Desert in the east. Seasons are extreme, and the harsh heat of summer has a short, heavy rainy season. This challenging land has known few intruders. Perhaps this is why the Tjimba and Himba still practice much of their traditional culture and lifestyle.

In the mid-eighteenth century, a section of

The distinctive dress of Herero women, such as these Mbanderu women from Botswana, has become a symbol of Herero culture. Tourists now buy dolls costumed with all the proper details of dress, including several petticoats. Some say that the bulky dress makes women walk with the slow dignity of cattle; a very positive image for pastoralists like the Herero, who treasure their herds. The headgear of the costume is also like the wide horns of African cattle.

THE HERERO LONG DRESS

Many Herero women wear long cloth dresses with many petticoats underneath, and matching headdresses. These outfits are regarded as proper dress for traditional married women. By wearing the "long dress," a newly married woman shows her in-laws that she is willing to take up the responsibilities of a Herero home and will raise her children to respect their heritage and their father's family.

The long dress is heavy, hard to keep clean, and laborious and expensive to make. The outfit has changed over the years to reflect the style of new generations, and sewing it allows women to show their personal skill and creativity.

The Herero women's long dress has become a symbol of Herero tradition for Herero, tourists, scholars, and other Namibians. Women have thus become key symbols of the strength of Herero culture and the struggles of the Herero past. They play an important role in public life, representing the ideals of Herero culture: individualism blended with co-operation; respect for family and the past; and group unity.

Women are now selling dolls, wearing exact replicas of the long dress, to tourists and crafts organizations. This suggests that they continue to find new ways to express their individual and traditional identities.

the Kaokoveld population migrated to central Namibia and met up again with the Mbanderu. The people who undertook this migration became known as the Herero, and they are the focus of this book.

The traditional Herero idea of land ownership was that wherever they grazed their cattle was their land. Thus Hereroland is a vague concept,

because land occupied by the Herero bands of nomadic pastoralists never had fixed boundaries. When the Herero migrated into central Namibia, they eventually displaced Damara and Nama nomads with whom they competed for grazing land, particularly in times of drought. They frequently launched cattle raids into each other's territory. The Herero even tried raiding Ovambo territory in the north.

Around 1800, seven or eight Herero groups ranged across the area of Namibia lying between the Ugab, Swakop, and White Nossob rivers. At this time the Herero probably did not have hereditary chiefs, but followed charismatic leaders in family groups in a nomadic search for grazing.

Rival Herero chiefs were in the central plateau areas of Otjimbingwe, Okahandja, Omararu, and in parts of the Waterberg region. The Mbanderu settlements, situated around the well-watered Gobabis area, were also part of Hereroland. Hereroland occupied most of the best grazing land in Namibia. This made it an attractive target for colonial forces from Germany and Great Britain.▲

chapter

2

RELIGION AND BELIEFS

AS WITH MANY AFRICAN PEOPLES, PRECOLONIAL Herero religious beliefs are today combined with Christianity. To some extent religious practices and other aspects of culture are always changing. Therefore some Herero would not agree with all of the ideas that are discussed here as if they continued exactly as they were when European observers recorded them. Instead, these Herero may regard these as traditions that are more part of their history than of everyday life.

Today the majority of Herero and Mbanderu belong to Christian and Christian-inspired churches, particularly the Oruwanu Church among the Herero, and the Church of Africa among the Mbanderu. Nevertheless, most Herero still place great emphasis on the spiritual

importance of ancestors, and the same is true of many Christian Africans elsewhere.

Herero traditionalists believe in a supreme being called Njambi Karunga. All life comes from him. He lives in the heavens and is all-knowing. Njambi Karunga is the giver of all blessings, revered for his kindness. Most Herero today would identify him as God in the Christian religion.

The Herero believe that every individual possesses a soul that survives death to become the powerful entity called an ancestor, or *omukuru* (pl., *ovakuru*). The control that ancestors have over life is far-reaching, but the importance of departed souls diminishes with time and ultimately vanishes. The longer an ancestor is dead, the less he or she is remembered and appealed to.

Ancestors are the focus of traditional Herero religion. The *ovakuru* watch over their living relatives if they are treated correctly but cause misfortune if they are displeased. Therefore, the Herero are careful to maintain close and proper relationships with *ovakuru*.

In the religious practices that focus on ancestor reverence, a key element is Mukuru. Mukuru is a complex idea. It is an honorific term that can refer to ancestors as well as the living representatives of those ancestors in each family. There are four kinds of Mukuru: the

A family religious leader from near Okakarara, Namibia, stands at the sacred hearth of his family.

founding ancestor from which the family line originates; the most recent ancestor of a family; the head of the family, who is the living link between the family and its ancestors and acts as family priest; and the Christian God. The fact that the word Mukuru refers to both living and departed people shows how the ideas of ancestors and descendants are connected.

The male head of the household is its spiritual leader and a direct descendant of the ancestors. The Mukuru's main role is to intervene when evil threatens. He is also the channel through which his people can ask for blessing from their ancestors.

The physical focus of Herero worship is *omuriro omurangere*, the sacred fire. This is the symbolic link between the living and the dead. *Omuriro omurangere* is a gift from the lineage Mukuru, the original ancestor of the family line.

Herero religion operates on the understanding that life is a gift from the ancestors, and the fire symbolizes this gift. To maintain a good relationship with the ancestors, every household should always keep a sacred fire burning between the house of the Mukuru's first wife and the cattle kraal. Stones or a thorn hedge separate the sacred fire from its surroundings. An arrangement of cattle horns left after ritual sacrifices are kept near the altar on which the fire burns. A branch of the sacred tree *omumborombonga* is kept nearby to represent the ancestors.

According to Herero belief, certain people and objects are holy or untouchable, *zera*. There are behavioral rules or taboos regarding these people and objects. The household Mukuru and his saliva are *zera*, as are a woman about to give birth and her house; twins; the sacred fire and its hearth or *okuruuo*; certain parts of cattle; a grave and the objects on it; and the umbilical cord of a baby. If someone violates these taboos by words, deeds, or looking at them, he or she commits an offense against the ancestors. The many *zera* objects associated with daily life and the cycle of life assure that the ancestors are frequently remembered.

Although the Herero use milk and milk products from their cattle, such products are also surrounded by taboos. Many cattle are considered sacred; and certain kinds of *zera* cattle

This Mbanderu woman from Kuke in Botswana is transferring milk from a gourd. Cattle and cattle products are of great physical and spiritual importance to Herero. *Omaere* (sour milk) has a special significance. In the past, during a daily ceremony, *omaere* was poured from calabashes and taken to the family head for tasting before it was consumed by others. Today this ceremony is no longer regularly practiced by all Herero-speakers.

may be owned only by certain people. The use of their milk and meat is limited to the owners and particular relatives of the owners.

Fresh milk is poured into calabashes to sour, after which it is called *omaere*. When the milk has thickened, the curds and whey are brought to the Mukuru to taste before the rest of the household uses it. This ceremony was once a daily event but it is no longer practiced everywhere. *Omaere* is *zeri*, and it was once taboo to use *omaere* that had not been tasted by the household Mukuru.

According to early records of Herero tradition, a person who is sick or suffering misfortune may have offended an ancestor. Those who need to appease an ancestor must go to the *ombetere*, a diviner, for help. By contacting the ancestors, the diviner can find out what offense was committed. Thereafter, steps toward purification can begin. The first step is the purification offering. The supplicant brings his or her offering to the diviner, who sprinkles a mouthful of holy water over the wrongdoer and speaks to the ancestors about the transgressions of the supplicant. Then he pleads for forgiveness on behalf of his client. In especially difficult times this offering is not enough and the offended ancestor's grave must be visited in person for a more direct prayer. Only the family Mukuru or his appointed messenger can make this prayer.

Although many Herero customs and traditions have changed, Herero children often still wear leather aprons.

In some cases the services of herbalists are needed. They are experts in combining natural and supernatural powers. Appealing to the supernatural, they might make a healing balm from plants, or cause rain to fall.

Today, many Herero do not observe these traditional religious practices. Many of the old customs and beliefs are forgotten and are no longer part of the intricate fabric of social life. Among all the Herero speakers, the Himba and Tjimba are the most devoted to these traditions today.▲

chapter

3

SOCIAL ORGANIZATION AND CUSTOMS

EVERY HERERO BELONGS TO TWO CLANS: THE *oruzo,* or patriclan, of his or her father and the *eanda,* or matriclan, of the person's mother. Herero legend states that all Herero-speakers are descendants of the six virgin daughters of Mukuru and Kamangarunga, who founded the Herero matrilineal clans named after them: Omukwendata, Omukweyuva, Omukwenambara, Omukwante (or Omukwandongo), Omukwatjivi, and Omukwendjandje. The *eanda* is very important. It regulates key social institutions such as inheritance and marriage.

There are about twenty Herero *otuzo* (plural of *oruzo*). Unlike the *omannda* (plural of *eanda*), they do not have a legend about their source or common origin. The *otuzo* bear the names of animals such as the kudu (an antelope) and the chameleon. Each *oruzo* has its own set of reli-

In the past, and still for many Herero today, life revolved around cattle. This Mbanderu man in Botswana searches a group of stray cattle for one of his herd.

gious prohibitions that are obeyed by its members. These are mostly food taboos that forbid, for example, members of the kudu *oruzo* from killing or eating this animal. Members of the *otuzo* tend to live with or near each other, and they are made up of several family lines. The head of an *oruzo* is the spiritual and political leader of his clan and is honored by being called Mukuru. *Oruzo* leadership is passed from father to son.

Cattle are also part of Herero social structure, because they belong to the clan. Individual members of each clan own and use cattle in a caretaker-like capacity. Herero cattle belong to

23

two classes: the sacred cattle of the *oruzo,* and cattle held in trust by the *eanda.* The sacred herd of the *oruzo* is specially chosen for its excellence. The Herero set aside the finest cattle for sacrifice to their ancestors. The meat from these ceremonies is usually eaten. Some groups of Herero, however, will not eat meat from an ox sacrificed at a funeral. *Oruzo* cattle are inherited along the male line, while *eanda* cattle are passed from mother to daughter. *Eanda* cattle are used to pay family debts.

Again, while these aspects of Herero organization were observed by certain researchers in the 19th and early 20th centuries, they do not apply to all Herero today. However, relatives on the mother's and father's sides remain important. Generally, tradition remains stronger among rural Herero.

▼ HERERO SETTLEMENTS ▼

Until recently, ancestral worship formed the core around which Herero social structure and customs revolved. The Herero grouped themselves into homesteads settled around patrilineal relations. Generally, a collection of homesteads grew into a village, and the member families set up cattle outposts around the village. In this way they could pasture and water their herds without having to move along with them all the time.

The center of rural Herero settlements today

is the *onganda* or homestead, consisting of the dwellings of an extended family. This means that different generations live together as a family. All of them belong to the same *oruzo*.

The traditional Herero dwelling is now found only among the Himba and Tjimba. Many Herero and Mbanderu communities now have rectangular houses built with modern materials, but these are still often combined with traditional architecture.

A traditional homestead is constructed in a circular pattern. Furthest to the east is the house of the Mukuru's first wife. It is a special dwelling (*otjizero*) and holds all the sacred objects connected with ancestor reverence. To the right of the *otjizero* are all the dwellings of the adult sons, both married and unmarried. To the left of the *otjizero* is the area set aside for the dwellings of the Mukuru's other wives. The family's children and unmarried women stay here with their mothers. The homestead circle is completed by the dwellings of distant relatives and workers. In the middle of this circle, on the west side, is the cattle enclosure. The sacred fire of the homestead and its hearth (*okuruuo*) are kept between the cattle enclosure and the *otjizero*.

Women build and own the dwellings in a homestead, and men share the dwellings of their wives. The men usually help in cutting and collecting the poles and saplings used to construct

Few Herero build houses in the traditional style, but the patterns of the settlement have not changed much. Both these settlements continue to provide individual homes in the same *onganda* or homestead.

the framework of a dwelling. After the framework is set up to form a circular dome shape, it is plastered with a mixture of cattle dung and sand. The dwelling floor is also made of dung. When a dwelling is completed, it is referred to as *ondjuwo*.

Individual settlements grow as the men in a family marry. The *onganda* circle widens when it becomes the center of several satellite cattle outposts (*ozonganda*), which form the wider village unit of people belonging to a common *oruzo*.

The Herero have no tradition of centralized leadership or inherited positions of authority. Family leaders were followed because of their charisma and personal abilities, but if they disappointed the group an alternative relative in favor could come to occupy a leading role. As nomads generally intolerant of hierarchies, the Herero aimed to govern by consensus among the headmen of the various families within the group.

▼ SOCIAL LIFE ▼

For the Herero, cattle are part of the gift of life. Taking care of them is a serious business, and the rhythm of each day revolves around it. The men and boys are in charge of pasturing and watering the cattle and maintaining the cattle kraal; women and girls milk the cows in the mornings and evenings. After milking they prepare the *omaere* in the special calabashes re-

served for this purpose. These calabashes are never washed. When they break, new calabashes are prepared.

▼ BIRTH ▼

The Herero prepare for the birth of a child with great care. The expectant mother leaves her home and goes to stay with her mother. For the "lying-in" period, a woman from a well-to-do family usually has a special house built for her. This house is *zera*. No one may enter or use it after she leaves.

When a new baby's umbilical cord has fallen off, it is time to bring the infant to the village so that it can be welcomed. The naming ceremony is performed at the homestead of the maternal grandparents, during which the maternal grandfather presents a young cow to the new baby. The child's forehead is put against the cow's. This cow and any calves she may have now belong to the child. The child is given a name after the Mukuru sprinkles it and its mother with holy water that he holds in his mouth. The Herero always invent an original name for a child that usually describes a striking event at the time of its birth. The child also receives an English or an Afrikaans name during its childhood.

The mother returns to her husband's homestead when the name-giving ceremony is over.

Only now may the father see the new baby. At this time the child's maternal grandfather gives it another young cow. Friends and relatives also bring gifts for the child.

In the past, when a child grew his or her permanent teeth, the "tooth mark" ceremony was held at the sacred fire. A triangular notch was filed into the top front teeth and the four lower front teeth were knocked out. This seldom occurs today.

▼ MARRIAGE ▼

A man may not marry within his own matriclan. A marriage is negotiated between families. Sometimes boys and girls are "promised" to each other in early childhood.

A father always handles the engagement of his son. Marriage negotiations begin when a young man sends a string of beads to a young woman's family. If they are accepted, the two families can begin to talk. When the match is decided, it is sealed with the bridewealth in the form of cattle and sheep that a man gives his prospective in-laws. It is bridewealth that makes marriages official and children legitimate.

The traditional Herero marriage ceremony was in two parts, some elements of which are still followed today. The first part took place in the homestead of the bride's father. On the wedding day the groom came to the outskirts of the

Herero women are expected to wear the long dress to show their respect for their in-laws and for Herero tradition. These women attend a wedding in rural Namibia.

bride's village to present the bridewealth. He and his supporters waited there until the end of the ceremony. The wedding began with the slaughter of a young ox taken from the village. The bride's face was veiled throughout the wedding ceremony. After the slaughtering of more cattle the bride went to the sacred fire, where the *oruzo* leader blessed her with melted fat and holy water. Her mother then took her to a secluded place and removed her veil. The bride was now ready to join her husband.

The second part of the marriage ceremony took place at the groom's homestead. The bride and groom entered the groom's village at sun-

down with the bride holding the leather apron straps around her husband's hips. Groups of followers accompanied them on their tour of the village, each woman holding the straps of her husband's apron. The man who headed the procession knocked on each door in the village as they passed. He held out a basket when the door was opened and collected powder from a fragrant plant to present to the newlyweds.

According to custom, Herero men can have more than one wife, but this is now rare. Each wife had her own house. Looking after children and household tasks were the main duties of Herero women in the past, and this remains true in rural areas.

▼ DEATH ▼

Among the Herero, death is the time when a man goes to meet his or her ancestors. A family always sets aside some cattle for sacrifice at funerals. The cattle accompany the dead person on his or her journey to the ancestors.

The death of an important leader is a major event. A large sacrifice is made, consisting of cattle set aside for this occasion during his lifetime. Soon after the leader's death, his favorite ox is killed to provide the skin that serves as his burial shroud. Cattle are slaughtered in the following days and eaten during the funeral ceremonies. All cattle sacrificed for funerals are

Horns, usually of sacrificed cattle, are traditionally placed on the graves of important men. This recent grave of a family head near Maun is marked with kudu horns instead because they are the totem animal of the Ohorongo patrilineage to which he belonged.

slaughtered by suffocation, because blood must not be shed during the mourning period.

A man is buried with some personal items, and the grave is covered with earth and heavy stones. The horns of the cattle killed during the funeral are piled on or near the grave or bound to the tops of long wooden stakes. In earlier times many dozen cattle were sacrificed at leaders' funerals, and the sight of their graves was most impressive. These horns are a sign of the greatness of the dead person who is now among the ancestors. No one is allowed near the grave without being accompanied by a religious leader from the family of the deceased.▲

chapter

4

A HISTORY OF CONFLICTS

UNTIL THE END OF THE 1700S THE HERERO were a strong presence in central Namibia. At that time, however, a new force moved into the region occupied by the Nama. Orlam clans entered the south of Namibia, fleeing oppression by the Dutch settlers in the Cape area of present-day South Africa. The Orlam had guns and horses and organized themselves in a military fashion as they moved up into the center of Namibia, conquering and/or incorporating many groups of Nama people already living there.

In time the Nama formed an alliance with the strongest Orlam clan, the Afrikaners, under the leadership of Jonker Afrikaner, to protect their land and cattle. Jonker thought that it was only the Herero who stood in the way of his plans to control central and southern Namibia.

In 1830 the Herero were driven from

Otjomuise (today called Windhoek), their southernmost settlement, by Jonker. This started a period of Nama/Orlam dominance over the Herero. There were many bloody battles, and many Herero groups were captured.

The Herero never presented a united front against the newcomers. In 1842 some Herero chiefs temporarily joined the Nama/Orlam, believing this would help them in their struggles with other Herero chiefs over land and cattle. Chief Tjamuaha was the most important Herero to associate with Jonker. Together they controlled most of southern and central Namibia. Northern Namibia was unaffected by these events.

The informal alliance between Jonker and Tjamuaha lasted for almost 20 years (1842–1861). Acting partly as partners and partly as rivals, these leaders carried out frequent cattle raids on others. They traded cattle and other livestock with European colonists for guns, ammunition, and other goods. Within a generation the Herero possessed the guns that had given the Orlam their advantage, and they grew stronger. Tjamuaha's son, Maherero, was in charge of a special guard of armed Herero.

By the mid-19th century, European explorers, traders, and missionaries began to move into this area of central and southern Namibia. Some Orlam leaders had invited them to the territory

in the hope that they would strengthen trade between Namibia (then called South West Africa) and the Cape settlers. There was much tension between the inhabitants and the missionaries at this time. The missionaries had their own ideas about what their role should be, and they refused to submit to the authority of the chiefs. Several missionary societies were involved in the struggle for converts. They began to interfere in the politics of the territory. Missionaries and traders encouraged the Herero to attack the Nama/Orlam in a more organized fashion. Key battles were fought in 1864 and 1867.

In 1861 both Jonker Afrikaner and Tjamuaha died. Christian, Jonker Afrikaner's son, had been chosen to succeed them. After Christian, Tjamuaha's son Maherero was next in the line of succession. However, the Herero communities refused to support Christian Afrikaner. The opponents grouped themselves at Otjimbingwe, and Christian died in battle when he attacked the Herero there. After Christian's death, Maharero assumed leadership of the alliance, but Christian's brother challenged his authority. This period saw the crumbling of the unity of the Nama/Orlam communities, and the Herero gained superiority in the area.

By 1863 the informal alliance had ceased to exist. There were many skirmishes between the South West African communities, which weak-

Like many African peoples in the 1800s, the Herero both maintained their traditional leather dress and adopted Western clothing. Both these photographs of Herero-speakers were taken in 1876. Traditional hairstyles, leather cloaks, and pointed headdresses were worn by some Herero women (top) at the same time that the Mbanderu chief Aponda and his family were photographed in Western clothes (below).

HERERO DRESS IN THE 1800s

Until the mid-19th century, Herero people, like others in southern Africa, wore clothing made of leather. Men and children wore different kinds of leather aprons, and male heroes wore special pieces of animal fur and other ornaments. Adult women wore two leather skirt pieces around their waists, a long leather shawl decorated with iron beads, and a headdress with three points on top.

Like their African neighbors, the Herero began wearing European-style clothing in the 1850s, after European missionaries began to settle in southern Africa. Herero people saw rival Nama groups and missionaries wearing Western dress. Today items of Herero cloth clothing are still named after parts of the leather dress, suggesting that Herero people see continuity between the two types of dress.

Herero people still wear some of these old items of dress. Many children wear leather aprons when they are not in school. Men wear mostly store-bought clothes, but when they participate in the annual days of Herero cultural celebration they wear military-type uniforms and bits of animal fur.

ened their resistance to the European intruders in their territory. Maharero began to strengthen his ties with the Europeans, believing that they could help him gain control over all Hereroland. Very soon the Herero became a major force in central South West Africa. In 1880 was fought a major battle in which all the Nama chiefs opposed Maharero. In this battle the Herero were

the victors. By this time the Herero under
Maharero numbered more than 23,000.

▼ HERERO-GERMAN CONFLICT ▼

Meanwhile, without the knowledge of the
various South West African communities, the
British and Germans were deciding their destinies in Berlin. After the Europeans met to divide
Africa among themselves at the Berlin Confer-
ence in 1884, Germany won South West
Africa.

On April 24, 1884, German colonial authority in Africa officially began. The Germans established their presence on the coast and soon
moved inland as they began to consolidate their
occupation. They created individual "protection
treaties" with the local cultural groups, and this
opened the way for foreign intrusion into the
country. Many small indigenous groups traded
their sovereignty for German military support
against their neighboring rivals.

Chief Maharero signed a protection treaty
with the Germans in 1885, without consulting
other Herero chiefs. Maharero thought the
Germans could help him strengthen his political
power. Instead, more German settlers moved
into Hereroland. This created much tension between the Herero and the colonial government
and made Maharero break the treaty. However,
the damage had been done, and the Germans

increased their military might. Again, in 1890, Maharero accepted German protection. He decided that he could not fight both the Nama and the Germans.

By the time of Maharero's death in October 1890, the Germans had designated him Paramount Chief. The Germans supported Maharero's son, Samuel, in the struggle that arose over succession. Samuel's rise to leadership caused a deep rift among the Herero, because he overstepped the man whom the Herero themselves preferred.▲

A group of Herero men photographed in 1876.

chapter

5

EXILE

THE HERERO SOON CAME TO SEE THAT THEIR protection treaty with the Germans was actually bondage. The abuses of the European settlers against them soon included outright theft of Herero land and cattle.

In 1892 the Herero and Nama again tried to make peace so that they could form a united front against the Germans. The German government met this threat by increasing their use of military force in the region.

The turning point came in 1894 when Theodor Leutwein took command of the German colonial army in South West Africa. He subdued the smaller Nama communities and soon established a network of military bases all over Nama territory. In August 1894 he succeeded in a major attack on the most important Nama community.

Now the road north to Hereroland was open. Herero land and cattle had become a goal of the German colonists. After the defeat of the Nama they set about in earnest to take Herero territory. The Germans invented a southern boundary for Hereroland. Any cattle found outside this boundary were taken by the colonial authorities. The Mbanderu suffered most from this confiscation policy. The new southern boundary cut into their land. In March 1896 the outraged Mbanderu rebelled against the Germans.

Chief Kahimemua and Nikodemus Kambahahiza led the Mbanderu in the fight to regain their land. The Khaua, a Nama community, joined the Mbanderu in their resistance against the Germans. This rebellion was also a challenge to the authority of Samuel Maharero, whom the Mbanderu did not recognize as paramount chief.

The Herero did not support the rebellion. In fact, Samuel sought German support in the hope that it would help him achieve political control over all Hereroland. Samuel sold to German settlers much land in the well-watered areas of Hereroland. When his people complained, he soothed them with false promises that their land would soon be recovered. Personal ambition, opportunism, regional ambitions, and age-old animosities led him to help the Germans fight

the Mbanderu. Samuel and the Herero under him helped to suppress the Mbanderu uprising. In May 1896 the German authorities crushed the uprising and sentenced Chief Kahimemua and Nikodemus Kambahahiza to death.

Samuel Maharero had unwittingly delivered himself and his people into the hands of the Germans. With the Mbanderu out of the way, Leutwein turned his attention to conquering the remaining Herero.

▼ THE HERERO-GERMAN WAR ▼

As the colonial army cleared the way to the interior of German South West Africa, Germans settled on farms that the colonial government carved out for them from traditional Herero land. Not even Herero burial grounds were spared. In addition, the new settlers seized Herero cattle. In 1897 the Herero suffered yet another blow. A rinderpest epidemic destroyed 90 percent of the remaining Herero cattle. Unlike the German settlers, the Herero did not have cattle vaccines.

On January 12, 1904, the Herero could no longer stand by and watch as the settlers continued to steal their land and cattle. They rose up against these injustices. Samuel Maharero led them into battle. He called for a united resistance of all South West African communities

against the Germans. The Herero uprising became a rallying point in the resistance that Namibian communities began to wage against the German government.

The Herero entered the war with about 7,000 fighting men and scored many successes in the first eight months. They took the Germans by surprise and regained control over much of central South West Africa. To counter this, the Germans sent more troops into battle under the leadership of General Lothar von Trotha. Herero raiding parties were no match for the organized German military.

Von Trotha's goal was total destruction of the Herero. In August 1904 he launched a major attack. The Herero retreated to the Waterberg mountains, where their women and children sought refuge in camps. A fierce battle raged for two days at Hamakari. The German troops surrounded the Herero and massacred thousands with heavy weapons and artillery. Von Trotha had no intention of negotiating a peace agreement. He threw a cordon across the land to seal off all escape routes and issued a notorious "Extermination Order" that meant genocide for the Herero.

▼ DISPERSAL ▼

The battle of Hamakari was a disaster. The entire Herero population fled. Some fled into

VON TROTHA'S PROCLAMATION

Enraged by the Herero rebellion, General Von Trotha issued a proclamation that proved disastrous for the Herero:

"I, the great general of the German soldiers, send this letter to the Herero nation. The Hereros are no longer German subjects . . . I say to the nation: Any person who delivers one of the Herero captains as a captive to a military post will receive 1,000 Marks. The one who hands over Samuel will receive 5,000 Marks. All Herero must leave the country. If they do not, I will force them with cannons to do so. Within the German borders, every Herero, with or without weapons, with or without cattle, will be shot. I no longer shelter women and children. They must either return to their people or they will be shot at. This is my message to the Herero nation."

The following day he explained his plan in a letter. This is some of what he said:

"I believe that the nation as such should be annihilated, or, if this is not possible, they must be expelled from the country. This will be possible if the waterholes from Grootfontein to Gobabis are occupied. The constant movement of our troops will enable us to find the small groups of the nation who have moved back westward and to destroy them gradually."

Because his army did not have enough supplies, the Germans could not pursue the fleeing Herero and annihilate them, but Von Trotha later states in this letter that he has left the Herero only the options of perishing in the desert or trying to cross the border into present-day Botswana.

the more remote mountains; some went north-ward into Ovamboland. Many died in the desert trying to cross the border into Botswana. Samuel Maherero's followers fled east into the desert and went into exile in that country.

Von Trotha's policy of genocide was so suc-cessful that by 1905 about 75 to 80 percent of the Herero population had been wiped out through war and starvation. From 70,000, the Herero population fell to about 16,000.

Those Herero who remained in South West Africa faced a deliberate policy of the colonial government to disperse the Herero people. The Herero could no longer own land and cattle. They had nowhere to live and no means of live-lihood. They became refugees in their own country. Many of them were held as prisoners of war. The government forced men, women, and children to work for the German settlers. They broke up families by sending husbands, wives, and children to work in places far apart from each other. A man might not see his wives or children for many years at a time.

The land that formerly belonged to the vari-ous South West African communities now came under complete control of the Germans, who called the area a Police Zone. The Germans issued many repressive laws and regulations gov-erning the social and economic lives of the peo-ples of South West Africa (SWA).

▼ SOUTH AFRICAN OCCUPATION ▼

After Germany's defeat in World War I, the League of Nations (which later became the United Nations) seized all German colonies. In 1915 the League assigned to Great Britain the task of overseeing South West Africa. South West Africa was put under the supervision of South Africa, which was part of the British Commonwealth.

A long period of South African occupation and domination began. The South Africans continued the Germans' colonial policies and adapted them to their own program. They set out to make sure that indigenous people would have a difficult time surviving unless they participated in the labor programs of the government. South Africa imposed apartheid, built military bases in SWA, and exploited SWA's resources.

South African rule was strongly opposed by the people who endured it. Both peaceful and violent rebellions began after 1948, when the South African Nationalist Party came to power on an apartheid platform.

Under apartheid the Herero and other Namibian peoples were forced to live in ethnic reserves created by the South African government for the local population. The Herero were dispersed among the reserves of Ovitoto, Otjituuo, Aminuis, Epukiro, Waterberg-East, and

Otjohorongo. Some of them were also resettled in the inhospitable Kaokoveld.

Life was difficult on the reserves and living conditions very poor. It was almost impossible for traditional social structures to function properly. Men had to leave the reserves for long periods in search of wage-paying jobs. This was the only way that they and their families could survive. The land on the reserves was too poor to provide more than a meager harvest. The people could graze their cattle only around the scarce boreholes (deep, narrow wells) that served as the main source of water.

Meanwhile the Herero who had gone into exile in the neighboring country of Botswana had established separate Herero communities scattered among the local Tswana population. They resumed much of their traditional lifestyle, but the Tswana influenced them in many ways, for example in combining pastoralism with agriculture. In spite of all these changes, the Herero continued to retain a strong sense of their identity and still do so today.▲

chapter

6

SOCIAL AND POLITICAL CHANGES

THE MANY CONFLICTS BETWEEN THE HERERO and their neighbors also played a role in the social and political changes in their national life. The years following the 1904 war with the Germans saw an increasing erosion of traditional Herero social structures and customs. The Herero were deprived of their land and their means of livelihood. Survival meant working for white farmers or in the many colonial labor camps attached to mines, railways, and diamond fields.

In 1961 South Africa became a republic and broke away from the British Commonwealth so that it could continue its apartheid policies. Human rights violations increased in South Africa and SWA. In the late 1960s many of the reserves for the indigenous populations were merged with new areas of land to create "home-

lands." The South African government claimed that the "homelands" were based on the regions traditionally settled by each people. Not only was this not true, but the best farming and grazing lands were not returned to their earlier inhabitants, and wage labor remained the only means of survival for many. The new Herero "homelands" did not include rights to the lush highlands they had once used for pasture.

▼ SOCIAL AND ECONOMIC LIFE ▼

The Herero slowly began to take control over their lives within the social and economic limitations of the homeland system imposed on them by the South African government. The realities of their environment meant that many of their traditional ways changed. Nevertheless, the Herero held on to the fundamental social structures that had traditionally given them a sense of social cohesiveness.

In the early years of social crisis, Christian churches became places where many Herero could come together and feel a sense of national identity. Although the Herero in central Namibia have a history of missionary contact, it was only around the turn of the century, when there was a breakdown in the cohesiveness of their national life, that Christianity was integrated with or became an alternative to ancestor reverence, *okurangere.*

Cattle remain an important part of Herero life. This man is a successful rancher in Botswana.

As Christianity took hold, the traditional practice of *okurangere* acquired a purely symbolic status among most Herero. Many Herero and Mbanderu who still find the sacred fire important do not tend it in the manner of their forebears. Usually only a few stones are placed in the traditional position reserved for the sacred fire. It is only during important community events that people gather at this spot, and sometimes light the fire. Many other customs that are closely tied to the practice of *okurangere* have also changed.

Cattle continue to be an important symbol of life to the Herero. They are still the mainstay of economic life, and the ownership of cattle is still

regarded as a status symbol. In spite of other means of livelihood that have been more available to the Herero through education and training programs, most Herero prefer to be cattle-farmers. However, their traditional pastoral lifestyle is no longer strictly followed. Even the Himba and Tjimba, who continue to observe many of the traditional Herero customs, now combine their pastoral ways with subsistence agriculture.

▼ POLITICAL ORGANIZATION ▼

The 1920s began a period of increased sociopolitical awareness and struggle among the Herero. During this time the Herero nation found an anchor in the person of Chief Hosea Kutako. When Samuel Maharero fled to Botswana he appointed Hosea Kutako to take his place among the Herero who remained in SWA (Namibia). Hosea Kutako came to represent a national political leadership for all Herero.

The national leader of the Herero confers with the Herero Council (*Ombongarero yomuhoko*) before he can take a final decision on any matter. *Ombongarero yomuihoko* is the highest authority in Herero politics today. It elects the Herero national leader.

An important social and political association arose among the Herero in 1923 at the time of the burial of Samuel Maharero. This was the

Every year on August 26, Herero loyalists gather at Okahandja in an impressive show of solidarity. Shown is the gathering of 1988.

Red Band or Red Flag Organization (*Otjira tjotjiserandu*), organized along military lines. On August 26, 1923, when Samuel Maharero's body was brought to Okahandja for burial among his ancestors, the Herero nation gathered. In the years that followed, the anniversary became a day of assembly and inspiration for Herero people.

A mass ceremony is held at Okahandja each year on August 26 at the burial places of the Herero chiefs. There are now three Bands, known as the Red, Green, and White Bands, or Flags. Each flag honors different lineages of ancestors and heroes. They gather annually at different grave sites in Namibia and Botswana. The Herero use these annual pilgrimages to reaffirm their social unity. This demonstrates that ancestor reverence is still a living part of Herero life, and that the flame of their national sacred fire has not died out.

At the annual Okahandja gathering, the three Flags unite. The women at left are from the Red, Green, and White Flags.

Flag ceremonies combine ancestor veneration with military-style parading and uniforms. All the ceremonies include camping near an important grave, sharing food, praise songs, dancing, marching, horse-back riding, prayers, appeals to the ancestors, and speeches. At Mbanderu Green Flag ceremonies, participants may also visit important religious specialists to be healed of physical ailments. At all the ceremonies, the climax is the moment when the participants file past the graves to attract such ancestors' blessings as health, fertility, and prosperity.

Each flag has many "troops" associated with particular towns, villages, or schools. Those who belong to the troops are required to wear uniforms that both mark the loyalty of committed troop members and emphasize the unity of the whole group. Typically, men wear a stiff shirt or jacket, trousers, a hat, and a belt. These may be ordinary store-bought clothes but tend to be

military in style. Teenaged boys wear the kind of short-sleeved shirts and shorts that they wear to school.

On all the uniforms, one's affiliation to a particular flag is expressed in the use of color. Most men wear khaki-colored clothes with small pieces of fabric in the color of their flag attached to their hatbands, upper sleeves, cuffs, or epaulettes. In Herero these colored badges are called *ovihako* (pl.) or earmarks, as in those given to cattle.

Military-style ranks and decorations are awarded to outstanding troopers by the highest-ranking flag leaders. Crowns, crossed swords, and stars and stripes associated with particular ranks are then worn on members' colored badges. Rank is also recorded in the trooper's personal membership book, in which participation in a ceremony is recorded with a stamp.

Women march in the troops but are positioned behind the men in the line; women can achieve rank, but not at the highest levels, and cannot do the most important things such as leading the troops to the graves and speaking to the ancestors at the graves.

However, women's uniforms provide the most impressive expressions of flag unity. The basic parts of the woman's uniform include a long dress (*ohorokweva onde*), like those that many Herero women wear every day, together with a

special jacket or a blouse for troop celebrations. They may also wear badges of rank on their sleeves.

The ideal woman's uniform is one in which all the dress, headdress, and accessories are co-ordinated in green, white, or red to match the colors of the three flags. The parade of uni-formed marchers making their way to the graves of their ancestors is a powerful sight, and the uniforms of women with their voluminous fabric of matched color, usually 10 yards or more, is especially impressive.

The uniforms symbolize the fact that every marcher is both a recognized community leader and a group member. Troopers are role models, and when all the uniformed troops march in unison in a huge procession to the graves, the strength of the Herero community is made vis-ible both to the Herero and to the many onlook-ers who watch the ceremonies each year.▲

chapter

7

THE ENDURING FLAME

IT MAY BE SAID THAT EVERY TIME THE
symbolic flame of Herero sacred fires was relit,
their burning desire for freedom was reaffirmed.

The Herero played an important part in the
liberation struggles of Namibians, from soon
after their defeat by the Germans in 1904 and
throughout the struggle for freedom from South
African rule.

Chief Hosea Kutako's leadership inspired
organized national resistance to South African
rule. On March 18, 1949, he sent a cable to the
United Nations, communicating to the world
Namibians' desire for independence.

An English priest, the Rev. Michael Scott,
traveled to Namibia and collected petitions from
Namibian communities. From 1946 to the
1960s he presented these petitions to the UN on

behalf of Namibians. This was one way that the voice of Namibians was heard abroad.

Chief Hosea Kutako announced the formation of the Oruuano (Unity) Church on August 25, 1955, a day before the annual Herero pilgrimage to Okahandja. During the struggle for Namibian freedom, such independent African churches were very influential. They provided platforms for Namibian communities to speak out about their grievances.

The resistance movement gathered momentum as Namibians became aware of other liberation struggles. The ANC (African National Congress) in South Africa proved an important influence. Soon there were Namibian organizations like SWASB (South West African Students Body), SWAPA (South West African Progressive Association), and SWANU (South West African National Union). The late 1950s saw the rise of organized protest among trade unions in Namibia. Men like Toivo ya Toivo, Sam Nujoma, and Clemens Kapuuo led the resistance struggle.

In 1960 the need for a broad-based political organization was recognized. Namibians needed to fight not only the repressive labor system in their country, but colonialism itself. On April 19, 1960, SWAPO (South West Africa People's Organization) was founded, based on Marxist tenets. Sam Nujoma became its president. Peasants, students, workers, church leaders, and

After many years of armed struggle, the South West African People's Organization (SWAPO) came to power. Here a SWAPO rally in Windhoek prepares for the first democratic elections in Namibia.

even traditional leaders joined SWAPO. SWAPO introduced the name "Namibia" to its followers. Soon it replaced "South West Africa," and everyone called their country Namibia. The new name symbolized a new national identity. The United Nations General Assembly officially recognized Namibia as the name of the country.

The liberation struggle waged by SWAPO soon became a prolonged armed struggle in which Namibian communities made great sacrifices. Many Namibians turned to guerilla warfare and settled communities provided rural bases from which fighters could attack the South African army. SWAPO was supported by many other Afri-

can countries. The international community, in the form of the UN, was also greatly involved in planning Namibia's freedom from South Africa.

The 1970s and 1980s were a period of increased political and military resistance. Slowly, the Namibians eroded the colonial power of South Africa. People from all spheres of life became involved in the fight.

▼ NAMIBIA IS FREE ▼

The journey to independence ended as the South African flag came down at midnight on March 20, 1990. The hearts of Namibians lifted as they watched their flag rise. Yet, in this moment of happiness, many knew that the struggle had not ended. A new phase was about to begin.

The SWAPO government under Sam Nujoma faces a difficult task in trying to live up to the expectations of the people and restore fundamental human rights. There is still a wide gap in social conditions among Namibians, but there is optimism for the future.

Their struggle for independence has helped the different Namibian communities understand that their destinies are linked. The future lies in Herero, Nama, Ovambo, Damara, and others coming together with their different heritages to build a united Namibia.▲

In both Namibia and Botswana, Herero-speakers form part of multiethnic countries in which cooperation is important for national stability. At the Botswana Independence Day anniversary celebrations shown here, two Herero headdresses stand out.

Glossary

eanda Matriclan; relatives on the mother's side.

genocide Attempted destruction of an entire cultural group.

kudu Species of antelope.

okurangere Ancestral reverence.

okuruuo Sacred fire and hearth.

ombetere Diviner.

omaere Curdled, sour milk.

omuriro omurangere Sacred fire.

onganda Homestead.

ondjuwo Dwelling.

oruzo Patriclan; relatives on the father's side.

otuzo Patriclans (plural).

otjizero Home of the priest's first wife.

ovakuru Ancestors.

ovihuro Village.

ovitunga Bridewealth.

ozonganda Homesteads (plural).

taboo Forbidden act or behavior.

zera Holy persons and things.

For Further Reading

Banister, Anthony, and Johnson, Peter. *Namibia: Africa's Harsh Paradise*. London: Country Life Books, 1979.

Bridgman, Jon. M. *The Revolt of the Hereros*. Berkeley: University of California Press, 1981.

Katjavivi, P. *A History of Resistance in Namibia*. London: John Currey, 1988.

Pendleton, W. *Katatura: A Place Where We Do Not Stay*. San Diego: San Diego University Press, 1974.

Index

ABOUT THE AUTHOR
Ada Udechukwu was born in Enugu, Nigeria. She holds a bachelors degree in literature from the University of Nigeria, Nsukka. She is currently a full-time artist and writer and has taken part in several exhibitions within Nigeria. She is the author of a collection of poems, *Woman Me*.

ACKNOWLEDGMENTS
The publishers gratefully acknowledge the contribution of Dr. Hildi Hendrickson, who commented on the manuscript and provided the material on Herero dress (in the boxes on pp. 13 and 37) and on Herero Flag ceremonies (on pp. 52–55), drawing from material in her Ph.D. dissertation *Historical Idioms of Identity Representations among the Ovaherero in Southern Africa*, Ann Arbor: University Microfilms, 1992.

COMMISSIONING EDITOR: Chukwuma Azuonye, Ph.D.

CONSULTING EDITOR: Gary N. van Wyk, Ph.D.

PHOTO CREDITS
Cover, pp. 8, 12, 17, 23, 26 bottom, 30 by Hildi Hendrickson; pp. 19, 21, 26 top, 32, 50, 52, 53, 58 by Dean Jacobson; p. 60 by Elizabeth Ann Schneider; p. 36 top, p. 36 bottom, and p. 39 bottom, National Archives, Namibia, courtesy of Hildi Hendrickson.

DESIGN: Kim Sonsky